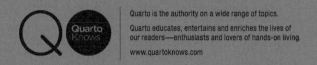

Quarto is the authority on a wide range of topics.

Quarto educates, entertains and enriches the lives of our readers—enthusiasts and lovers of hands-on living.

www.quartoknows.com

First published in the U.S.A. in 2017 by Wide Eyed Editions,
an imprint of The Quarto Group,
142 W 36th Street, 4th Floor, New York, NY 10018, U.S.A. QuartoKnows.com
Visit our blogs at QuartoKids.com

Important: there are age restrictions for most blogging and social media sites and in many countries parental consent is also required. Always ask permission from your parents. Website information is correct at time of going to press. However, the publishers cannot accept liability for any information or links found on any Internet sites, including third-party websites.

ISBN 978-1-78603-033-7

Illustrated digitally

Set in Fugue, Bebas Neue, and Futura

Published by Rachel Williams
Designed by Karissa Santos
Edited by Katy Flint
Production by Dawn Cameron

Printed in China

1 3 5 7 9 8 6 4 2

MIX
Paper from
responsible sources
FSC® C104723
FSC
www.fsc.org

ONE HUNDRED THINGS TO SPOT

WIDE EYED EDITIONS

HOW TO USE THIS BOOK

In this book there are one hundred things to spot. They are hidden in different places. Can you find them all?

COLORS IN THE JUNGLE

A white moth

An orange orangutan

A blue bird

A gray bush baby

A purple bug

A cat

A multicolored chameleon

And a little brown mouse!

1. SEE AND SAY EACH OBJECT.

2. TURN THE PAGE TO LOOK FOR THEM.

3. SHOUT AS YOU FIND EACH ONE.

An orange orangutan!

WHICH COLORS CAN YOU SPOT HERE?

4. CAN YOU FIND THE CAT AND MOUSE?

One bear

Two foxes

Three owls

Four
rabbits

Five
squirrels

A cat

And a little mouse!

Six rockets

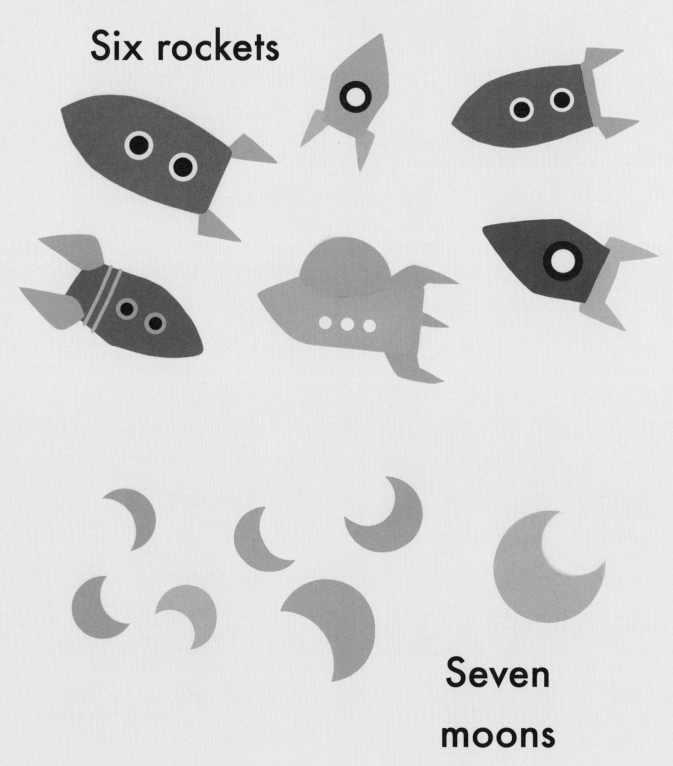

Seven moons

Eight planets

Nine space rocks

Ten stars

A flying cat

And a little mouse!

13

HOW MANY THINGS CAN YOU COUNT HERE?

15

A black-and-white cat

A black bird

A red ladybug

A green
frog

A yellow bee

A blue butterfly

A pink worm

And a little
brown mouse!

WHICH COLORFUL THINGS CAN YOU SPOT HERE?

19

A hot tea kettle

A sweet
strawberry

A cold
refrigerator

A salty
pretzel

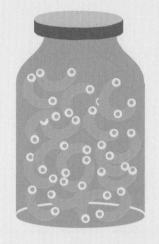

A full jar   An empty jar

A big cat

And a little mouse!

WHICH OPPOSITES CAN YOU SPOT HERE?

23

A starfish

 A spiral shell

A rectangular beach towel

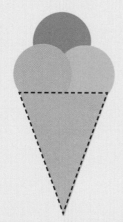 A triangular
ice-cream cone

A circular ring

A square
sand castle

A cat

And a
little mouse!

WHICH DIFFERENT SHAPES CAN YOU SPOT HERE?

27

THINGS AT THE CAFE

A bag under a table

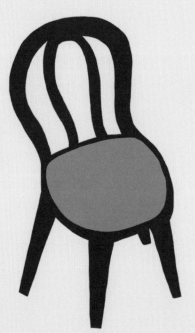

A chair behind a table

Sugar next to a cup

A cookie on a plate

28

A waiter in
front of a
blackboard

Flowers in
a vase

An umbrella
above
a table

A cat

And a little mouse!

29

WHICH THINGS CAN YOU SPOT HERE?

A dry dog

A wet dog

Some light bubbles

A heavy laundry basket

An open cupboard

A closed cupboard

A cat

And a little mouse!

WHICH OPPOSITES CAN YOU FIND HERE?

SIZES AT THE FAIRGROUND

A small ticket

 A big bear

 A short line

 A long line

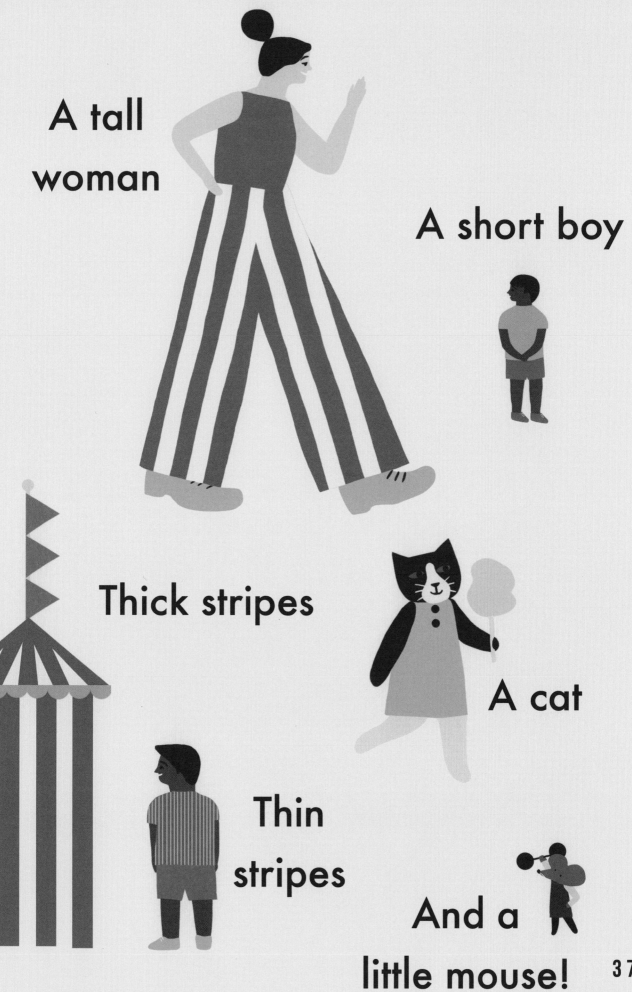

A tall woman

A short boy

Thick stripes

A cat

Thin stripes

And a little mouse!

37

WHICH SIZES CAN YOU FIND HERE?

OPPOSITES AT THE PARK

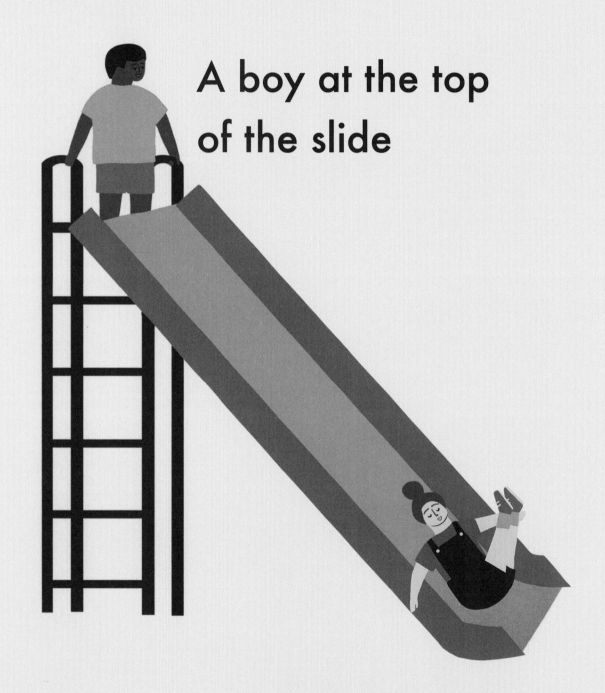

A boy at the top
of the slide

A girl at the
bottom of the slide

A slow snail

A fast bike

A bird on a high branch

A cat

A little mouse on a low branch!

WHICH OPPOSITES CAN YOU SPOT HERE?

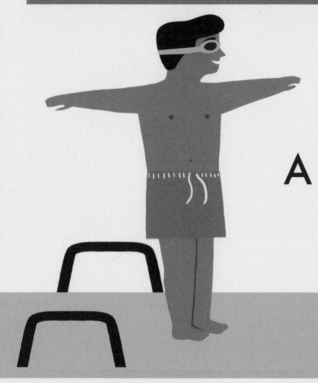

A hard diving board

A soft robe

A fluffy dog

A bumpy slide

A sticky
Popsicle

A furry cat

And a little mouse!

WHICH TEXTURES CAN YOU SPOT HERE?

A sad boy

A happy girl

A surprised girl

A shy child

48

An embarrassed
boy

An angry
chef

An excited cat

And a hungry
little mouse!

HOW ARE PEOPLE FEELING HERE?

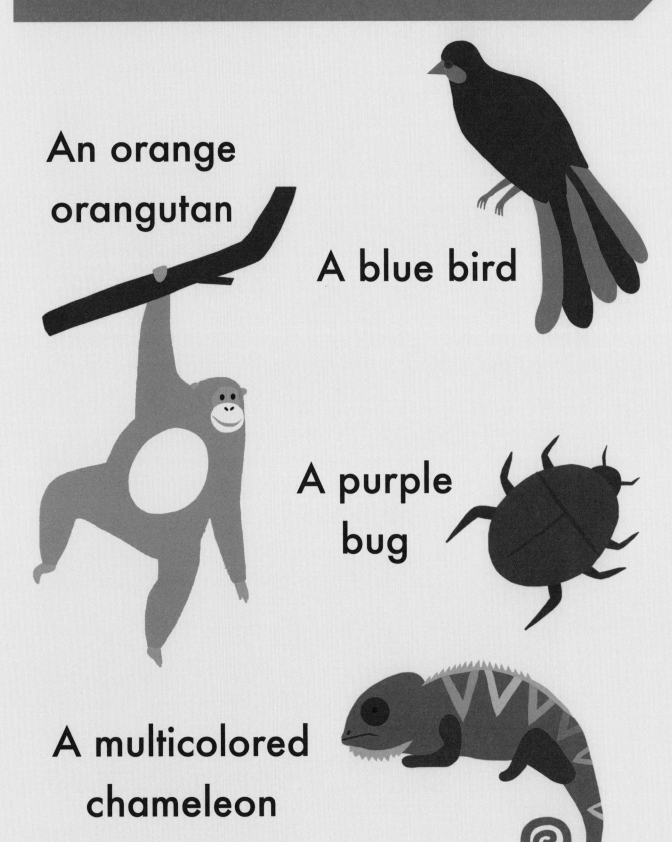

An orange orangutan

A blue bird

A purple bug

A multicolored chameleon

A white moth

A gray
bush baby

A cat

And a little
mouse!

53

WHICH COLORS CAN YOU SPOT HERE?

54

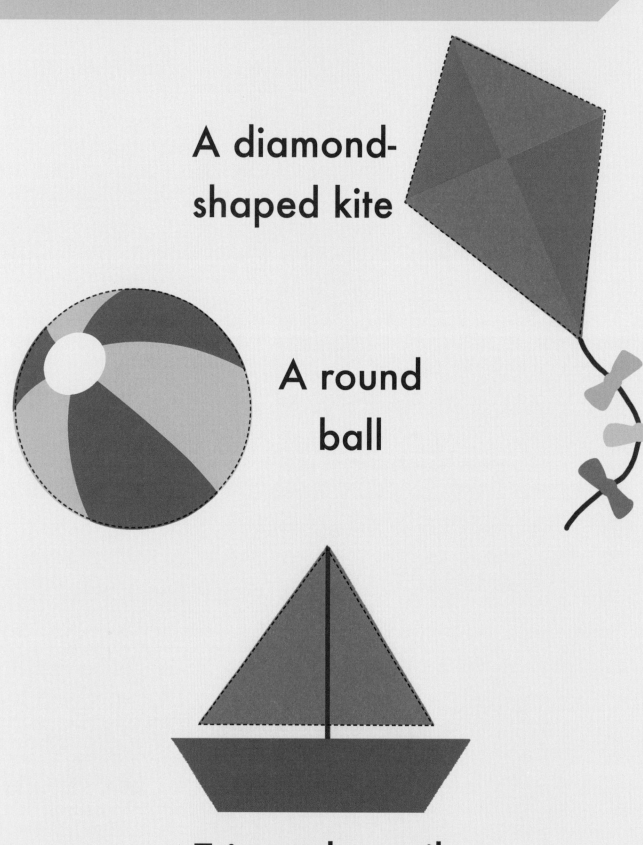

A diamond-shaped kite

A round ball

Triangular sails

Rectangular
blocks

A cat with a
square bag

A little mouse with
a heart lollipop!

WHICH SHAPES CAN YOU SPOT HERE?

A camouflaged
zookeeper

A zigzag
snake

A striped
tiger

A butterfly with
wavy wings

A speckled
egg

A spotted
leopard

A cat

And a little mouse!

WHICH PATTERNS CAN YOU SPOT HERE?

One triangular tent

A cat

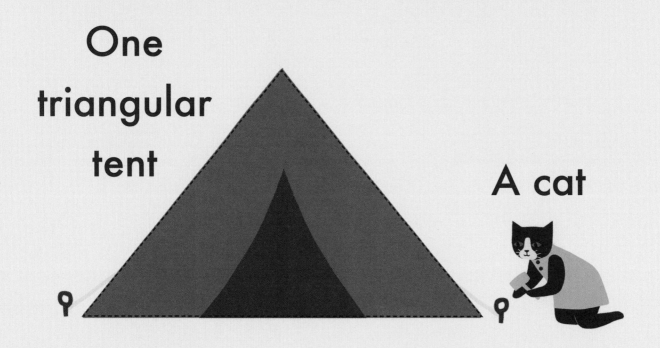

Two rectangular backpacks

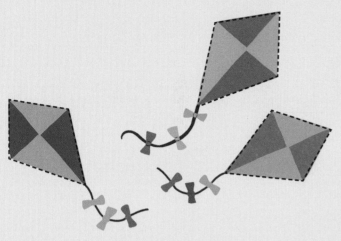

Three diamond-shaped kites

Four square lamps

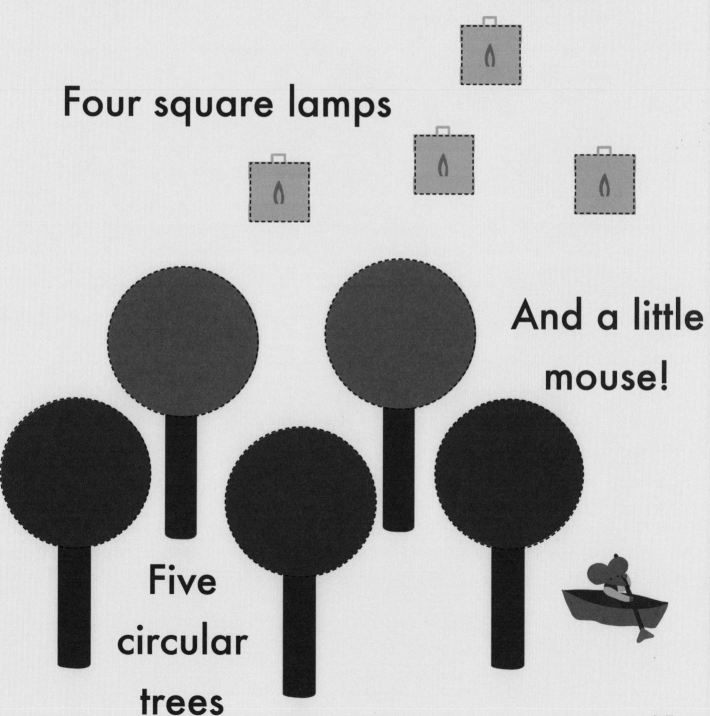

Five circular trees

And a little mouse!

HOW MANY SHAPES CAN YOU COUNT HERE?

Six green turtles

Seven pink jellyfish

Eight yellow fish

Nine
cream
shells

Ten
purple
plants

A cat

And a little
mouse!

69

HOW MANY COLORS CAN YOU COUNT HERE?

A bright moon

A dark sky

An awake cat

A shelf above
the bed

A sleeping girl

Roller skates
below the bed

And a little mouse!

WHICH OPPOSITES CAN YOU SPOT HERE?

HAVE YOU SPOTTED ALL ONE HUNDRED THINGS? WHICH ONE HAVEN'T YOU SEEN BEFORE?

ADMIT ONE